W9-BRC-835

To

Asher Ryan Adams

From

Patricia Leham

Date

_2016_

GOTTA HAVE GOD
FOR LITTLE ONES

My First Devotional for Toddler Boys Ages 2-3

Illustrated by
Olga & Aleksey Ivanov

ROSEKiDZ®

An imprint of Rose Publishing, Inc.
Carson, CA
www.Rose-Publishing.com

Gotta Have God For Little Ones, My First Devotional for Toddler Boys, Ages 2-3
©2016 Rose Publishing, All rights reserved.

Written by Mary Gross Davis
Contributing Editor: Cashmere Walke

RoseKidz®
An imprint of Rose Publishing, Inc.
17909 Adria Maru Lane
Carson, CA 90746
www.Rose-Publishing.com

Register your book at www.Rose-Publishing.com/register and receive
a free Bible Reference download.

Cover and interior design by Mary pat Pino
Illustrated by Olga and Aleksey Ivanov

Scriptures are from the New Revised Standard Version Bible, copyright ©1989 by the Division of Christian Education of the National Council of Churches of Christ in the U.S.A.
Used by permission. All rights reserved.

No part of this publication may be reproduced in any form, stored in a retrieval system, or transmitted in any form or by any means without the written permission of Rose Publishing.

Printed in South Korea
01   04.2016.APC

"To all children of God"
O. & A. I.

It's Good to Thank God

Ben was excited! Nana and Papa were at his house for a special Sunday dinner!

The family stood in a circle and held hands.

"Let's each tell God something we are thankful for," Dad said.

"I'm thankful for this warm day!" Papa said.

"I'm thankful for the yummy food we are about to eat!" Nana said.

Finally, it was Ben's turn. Ben didn't know what to say.

Papa grinned and said, "Ben, I am thankful for YOU. Are you thankful for ME?"

"YES!" Ben said. Then he said, "I am thankful for Papa! And Nana! And Mom and Dad!"

Everyone smiled at Ben.

Then they all said together, "Give thanks to the Lord, for he is good!"

Ben agreed, "You are GOOD, God! I am thankful for you!"

Talk About It

Who was at Ben's house? What day was it?

Who was Ben thankful for?

Who are you thankful for? Who loves and helps you? God gave that person to you!

Try This!

Play a clapping game together!

Say, "Give thanks (clap, clap)

to the Lord (clap, clap),

for He (clap, clap)

is good" (clap, clap).

Keep clapping and playing until you can all say the Bible verse!

Prayer

God, You are good to us.
Thank You for our families.
Thank You for food.
We love You!
Amen.

God's Words

Give thanks to the Lord, for he is good. (See Psalm 118:1.)

It's Good to Trust God

Lucas and his family were camping in their own backyard.

They were cooking dinner over a fire. It was fun, especially when they heard it POP and CRACKLE!

But then, Lucas heard a noise in the bushes.

He peered into the dark. He saw two EYES shining in the bushes. Lucas was SCARED!

"Papi! Papi! A MONSTER in the bushes!" he shouted.

Papi hugged Lucas and said, "Lucas, God will keep us safe. We can trust Him."

Papi and Lucas prayed. Lucas felt better.

Then Papi said, "Lucas, let's look and see whose eyes those are!"

"NOOO!" Lucas begged as Papi reached into the bushes.

Papi pulled out Tomtom, their CAT!

Tomtom said, "Meow!"

They all laughed.

"Tomtom is our friendly monster!" Lucas said.

Lucas and his family laughed and laughed!

Talk About It

What did Lucas see in the bushes?

How did Lucas feel?

Who will help us when we are scared?

Try This!

With your family, have a picnic in your living room or back yard.
Spread out a blanket to sit on. Bring some snacks and a drink.
Talk about times people get scared. Thank God for His help!

God, we are glad You are with us. We are glad You will help us. We can always trust You.
Amen.

God's Words

God is my helper. (See Psalm 54:4.)

It's Good to Help Others

Mason and his sister Emma were riding their bikes in the driveway.

"I can go FAST!" Mason said.

"I can go FASTER!" Emma laughed.

She zoomed past him. Then she yanked her bike wheel HARD.

Emma's bike fell sideways! She started crying. She scraped her knee!

Mason ran to Emma and hugged her.

"I'll get Mommy!" he said. He dashed into the house and pulled Mommy outside. When she saw Emma was hurt, Mommy carried her into the house. Mason held Emma's hand as Mommy washed Emma's knee. He helped put an airplane bandage on Emma's scrape.

"Thank you for helping your sister," Mommy said. "It's good to help people. It makes us happy. And it makes God happy too!"

Talk About It

How did Mason help Emma?

Name the people in your family. Who is bigger? Who is smaller?

Say one way you can help a person in your family.

Try This!

With a bigger person, make a list of ways you can help at home. Put the list where you can see it. Every day, ask someone to read one way back to you—and then help in that way!

Prayer

God, thank You that we
can help each other!
Please help us to remember
to be good helpers.
Amen.

God's Words

One can help the other. (See Ecclesiastes 4:10.)

15

It's Good to Share

Ethan played with all the trucks in the sandbox. He was playing by himself when Sophia came to play. She reached for one truck.

"No!" Ethan grabbed the truck. "That's MY truck!"

"I need a truck too," Sophia said.

"No—they're mine!" he shouted.

Sophia looked sad.

"Can I please have one?" she asked.

Ethan didn't want to share. But Ethan remembered. He liked it when Sophia shared with him. He should share too.

So he picked up a truck and gave it to her.

"You can have a turn," he said.

"Thank you, Ethan," she smiled.

Soon, they were both zooming the trucks all over the sand.

Ethan was happy! Sophia was happy! And God was happy they shared.

Talk About It

Who shares with you?

How do you feel when someone shares with you?

What is something you like to share?

What is something you don't like to share?

Try This!

Play a sharing game together! Sit on the floor. Roll a truck back and forth to each other. Each time you roll the truck say, "I can share with you today. We take turns so we can play."

God, thank You that You share with me. Please help me to share, even when I don't want to.
Amen.

God's Words

Share with others. (See Luke 3:11.)

It's Good to Be Brave

Michael liked watching the birds fly in and out of the trees.

One day, he saw a baby bird. It flapped, flopped and flew down to sit on the grass.

But then, Michael saw his CAT, Linus. Linus's tail twitched as he crouched in the grass. Michael knew Linus was about to pounce on the little bird!

Michael stood in front of the baby bird and shouted, "Linus, no!"

Then he prayed, "God, help me keep the bird safe!"

Finally, the baby bird said, "CHEEP" and flew off!

Michael laughed. God had helped him keep the baby bird safe.

He felt happy! He felt brave and kind!

"Come on, Linus," said Michael. "I'll get you some CAT food!"

Talk About It

When has someone helped you?

When have you helped someone?

Who can help us to be brave and do what is right?

Try This!

Ask someone in your family to tell about a time when he or she had to be brave. Ask them to tell how it felt to be brave. Ask them to tell who helped them to be brave.

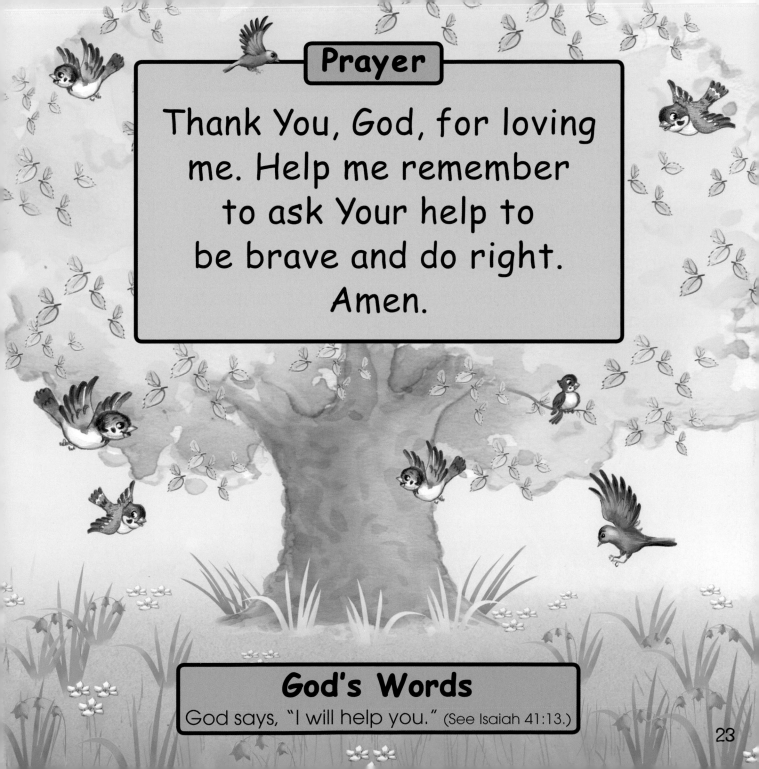

Prayer

Thank You, God, for loving me. Help me remember to ask Your help to be brave and do right. Amen.

God's Words

God says, "I will help you." (See Isaiah 41:13.)

It's Good to Show Love

When Daddy came home, Alex ran and gave him a HUGE hug.

Daddy smiled and said, "Hi Alex! How was your day?"

"I made a new friend, Jacob," Alex said. "He was mad at first because his twin sister was being mean. But I wanted him to be happy. So I showed him your trick!"

"What trick is that?" Daddy asked.

"I showed him to take deep breath and count to ten. I counted to ten with him. Then he calmed down. Now Jacob is my friend!" Alex said.

Daddy grinned. "Alex, the Bible tells us to show love to people and help them when they need it. You showed God's love to Jacob."

"Loving people makes me happy, too!" Alex said and grinned.

Talk About It

What did Alex do to show love?

What is a way you can show love to a person in your family?

What is a way you can show love to a friend?

Try This!

Ask a parent to help you think of two people you care about. Make "I love you" cards or drawings for them. Ask for help to mail or give the card to them. It will make their hearts happy and make your heart happy, too!

Dear God, thank You for showing love to me. Please help me do good things for people. I want to show Your love! Amen.

God's Words

Love each other. (See John 13:34.)

It's Good to Obey

Daniel and Grandma were on a walk when he spotted a puppy across the street!

He let go of Grandma's hand and jumped off the curb.

Grandma shouted, "STOP!"

Daniel STOPPED. A truck ZOOMED right past him!

"Thank you for listening, Daniel," Grandma said, giving him a hug. "That's why before we cross the street we stop, look, and listen. What else do we say?"

Daniel thought. "We say, 'OBEY RIGHT AWAY'!"

"That's right," Grandma said. "If you hadn't STOPPED when I said, 'Stop,' you could have been hit by that truck! That's why it's important to OBEY RIGHT AWAY!"

Daniel and Grandma crossed the street and petted the puppy.

"Thank you, God, for puppies!" Daniel said.

Grandma said, "Thank You, God, that Daniel OBEYED RIGHT AWAY!"

Talk About It

Why did Daniel start to run across the street?

What did Daniel do before he crossed the street?

What did Grandma and Daniel say about obeying?

What rules do you obey right away?

Try This!

Play this game with your parents. Take turns to give a direction like "touch your nose" or "turn around." Practice saying, "Obey right away!" as you do it. Talk about why it is important to OBEY RIGHT AWAY. Then march around the room while you repeat, "Obey right away!"

Dear God, thank You for people who love me and keep me safe. Please help me to obey right away. It's a good thing to do! Amen.

God's Words

Obey your parents. (See Colossians 3:20.)

32